Dear Parent:
Your child's love of reading starts here!

Every child learns to read in a different way and at his or her own speed. Some go back and forth between reading levels and read favorite books again and again. Others read through each level in order. You can help your young reader improve and become more confident by encouraging his or her own interests and abilities. From books your child reads with you to the first books he or she reads alone, there are I Can Read Books for every stage of reading:

SHARED READING
Basic language, word repetition, and whimsical illustrations, ideal for sharing with your emergent reader

BEGINNING READING
Short sentences, familiar words, and simple concepts for children eager to read on their own

READING WITH HELP
Engaging stories, longer sentences, and language play for developing readers

READING ALONE
Complex plots, challenging vocabulary, and high-interest topics for the independent reader

ADVANCED READING
Short paragraphs, chapters, and exciting themes for the perfect bridge to chapter books

I Can Read Books have introduced children to the joy of reading since 1957. Featuring award-winning authors and illustrators and a fabulous cast of beloved characters, I Can Read Books set the standard for beginning readers.

A lifetime of discovery begins with the magical words **"I Can Read!"**

Visit www.icanread.com for information on enriching your child's reading experience.

For Nathan and Luca.
Enjoy!
—R.S.

I Can Read Book® is a trademark of HarperCollins Publishers.

Library of Congress Control Number: 2014960374
ISBN 978-0-06-229422-7 (trade bdg.) —ISBN 978-0-06-229421-0 (pbk.)

16 17 18   PC/WOR   10 9 8 7 6 5 4 3   ❖   First Edition

I Can Read!

BEGINNING **1** READING

Splat the Cat
Twice the Mice

To: Brice Mouse
3 Cheddar Lane

Based on the bestselling books by Rob Scotton

Cover art by Rick Farley

Text by Jacqueline Resnick

Interior illustrations by Robert Eberz

HARPER

An Imprint of HarperCollinsPublishers

Seymour was sad.

He sighed.

He missed his brother, Brice.

So Seymour wrote a letter.

Dear Brice,

Would you like to visit?
We could play our favorite game,
Mice and Dice!

Your brother,

Seymour

Soon an envelope came in the mail.

It was from Brice.

It held one small slice of cheese

and one big message.

Brice was coming to visit!

DEAR SEY

THANK Y

Splat's tail wobbled with delight.
Seymour is a fantastic friend,
and now we'll have twice the mice!
thought Splat.

Splat couldn't wait

to tell his family.

"Guess what?" he said at breakfast.

"Seymour's brother, Brice,

is coming to visit tomorrow!"

9

"Cats do scare some mice,"

said Mom.

"Take my advice.

Be extra nice!"

"Let's make a sign
to welcome Brice,"
Splat said.
"We'll show him
that this cat is nice!"

All day long, Splat hustled,

and Seymour bustled.

They rented Brice's favorite movie,

Of Mice and Mice.

And they set up his favorite game,

Mice and Dice.

"This is more exciting
than fish cakes!" Splat said.
Seymour wrinkled his nose.
"And a slice of cheese,"
Splat added.

That night, Splat couldn't sleep.

Had he done enough to welcome Brice?

When Splat got up in the morning,

he paced the length of his room.

Once . . .

Twice . . .

Thrice . . .

"I know!" he said at last.

"I'll make a sculpture out of ice!"

Splat worked and worked.

He worked until his whiskers

were soggy.

Splat made two ice mice!

Splat didn't get much sleep,

but that was worth the price

to welcome Brice.

Splat and Seymour sat down to wait . . .

and wait . . .

and wait for Brice.

Seymour and Splat fell fast asleep.

Seymour's cheers woke Splat.

He saw a small gray mouse.

Brice was here!

SPLAT!

Seymour ran to hug Brice.

"Wait for me!" said Splat.

As Splat ran, he slipped
on the melting ice.

"Brice's gift!" said Splat.

His big gift for Brice

was now very small.

Splat was sad.

"It's mice-sized!" Brice said.

He posed with the ice sculpture.

"Thank you, Splat. You are

so nice."

Splat was glad.

"I have one more surprise," he said.

"Presenting Chef Splat," sang Splat,

"and his famous cheesy rice!"

"Yum!" Brice said

through a mouthful of rice.

When the cheesy rice was gone,

Seymour and Brice taught Splat

how to play Mice and Dice.

Splat gave his tail a happy wiggle.

"Twice the mice is twice as nice!"